Imago Christi

Exercises for Discovery Companions

Deepening Discovery with a Spiritual Companion

eds. Bill O'Byrne, John Pyrc & Kathy Pyrc

Exercises for Discovery Companions

TABLE OF CONTENTS:

Introductory Materials

Purpose

The *Exercises for Discovery Companions* are designed for people who have participated in an *Imago Christi* Spiritual Formation Discovery event to continue their journey of Discovery with each other. How do you intentionally live into your Longing for greater intimacy with God along the Timeline of your journey into deeper intimacy with God?

The *Exercises for Discovery Companions* are the fruit of both the work and the life of our *Imago Christi* Community in the Discovery themes. Our whole Community has worked together to create these Exercises, coming out of our own experience with the Discovery themes, and our experience in coaching other people through them. Our Community desires to help you continue to deepen your experience of the themes and practices introduced in the Discovery event long after the event is over.

If you have not experienced an *Imago Christi* Spiritual Formation Discovery event, please explore the possibility at your soonest convenience (www.imagochristi.org/discovery).

Jesus' prayer for us, as His disciples, was to first love the Lord with all our heart, with all our soul and with all our mind and strength, and then secondly, to love our neighbor as ourselves. Jesus desires that his followers experience communion in the Trinity, and community with one another (John 14:23; 17:20-23). Because we experience our unity with God *best* in spiritual community with other followers of Jesus, these Exercises have been designed for you to use, while engaged with another person, who has also experienced an *Imago Christi* Spiritual Formation Discovery event.

In this resource, you will find preparatory exercises for eight sessions that provide practical helps for you and your Discovery Companion to engage regularly in Abiding Prayer, and discover deeper insights about yourself, your spiritual journey, and your Longing for a more intimate relationship with God, so that you may intentionally live out your First Order Calling to love God first.

Discovery Companions Goals

- To gain deeper understanding of your identity in Christ and your journey of deepening intimacy with Him
- To deepen your experience of the Spiritual Formation Discovery themes in the spiritual community of Discovery Companions
- To develop your experience of spiritually formative community
- To support you in the continued development of your Spiritual Formation Plan.

Guidelines

- **Getting started:** Please read through these guidelines and pray about your participation in developing spiritual community using these Exercises with a Discovery Companion.

- **Selecting a Companion**: Given the nature of these Exercises, we suggest you meet in pairs. Both Discovery Companions should have already participated in an *Imago Christi* Spiritual Formation Discovery event. We encourage you to prayerfully seek and invite someone to take this journey with you. If you have trouble finding a companion, please contact us via email at: info@imagchristi.org. We will do our best to connect you with someone else who is looking for assistance in finding a potential Discovery Companion.

- **Length and Pacing:** The *Exercises for Discovery Companions* has been designed for you to go at your own pace and schedule. For example, the eight sessions could be completed in 8 weeks by meeting once a week or completed in 16 weeks by meeting every two weeks. We would not recommend letting your Discovery Companions experience go much longer than 20 weeks, or trying to complete more than one session in a single meeting.

- **Schedule Ahead:** Once you have found a Discovery Companion, choose a schedule that works best for you. To keep you working consistently together, we suggest that you schedule your meetings at least two meetings ahead.

- **Materials:**
  - o "Discovering Your Spiritual Formation Journey" workbook
  - o Discovery Pre-work
  - o Discovery Timeline
  - o Bible
  - o Personal journal for recording your exercise experience, and
  - o Calendar for scheduling.

Session Format

- **Opening Session**
- **Six Sessions** with Your Discovery Companion, including the following parts:
  - o Session Preparation:
    - Abiding Prayer Exercises
    - Deepening Discovery Exercises
  - o Discovery Companions Meeting:
    - Preparation reminders
    - Opening Prayer
    - Abiding Prayer Exercise
    - Sharing Insights
    - Mutual Support and Sharing
    - Closing Prayer
  - o Additional Resources.

- **Closing Session**

How to Use the Session Preparation Exercises:

- The Preparation work in each Session includes a section labeled "Abiding Prayer Exercises" and a section labeled "Deepening Discovery Exercises" to be completed *before you meet* for your Companions Meeting.

- Use the "Abiding Prayer Exercises" in place of your regular devotions, rather than overburden yourself. Do one Abiding Prayer Exercise based on one Scripture passage each time you do them.

- Refer to the "Four Movements of Abiding Prayer" below and start your Abiding Prayer Exercises according to the suggestions, utilizing the approach to prayer that works best for you, for example, *Lectio Divina*, or Ignatian Prayer.

- After a few days or weeks try to branch out to incorporate approaches that are less familiar to you, Wordless Prayer or Contemplation. In time, you may find yourself moving during a single Abiding Prayer Exercise from a form of active meditation, into more passive forms of prayer. There is no need to rush this process. This is a journey of a lifetime.

- Each Abiding Prayer Exercise can take between 30 to 60 minutes.

- Plan to do as many of the "Abiding Prayer Exercises" as is feasible in your schedule between Discovery Companions Meetings, so that you have time for the "Deepening Discovery Exercises" that you will be discussing in your Companions Meeting.

- Likewise plan enough time to do the "Deepening Discovery Exercises" in addition to the "Abiding Prayer Exercises." The time you spend on *each* of the "Deepening Discovery Exercises" will be a minimum of 30 minutes. Pick and choose *at least two* of the "Deepening Discovery Exercises" to complete, if you are meeting *every* week. Do *more, if not all,* of the "Deepening Discovery Exercises", if your meetings are further than a week apart.

- Take note of your experiences and insights from these Exercises in a personal journal. Mark in advance the points that you would like to share with your Companion during your Discovery Companions Meeting.

- We recommend that you not try to accomplish other aspects of the Spiritual Formation Plan that you developed at the end of Discovery, while engaging in the *Exercises for Discovery Companions*. Let the Discovery Companions experience serve as your Spiritual Formation Plan, which these Exercise will help you refine for use after you have completed the *Exercises for Discovery Companions*.

How to Facilitate the Discovery Companions Meetings.

- Please allow two hours for each Meeting with your Companion.
- Make sure you have agreed upon the venue, or a video conferencing app, and are technologically prepared for the Meeting at least five minutes in advance.
- Make sure you have a back-up plan to communicate, if your computer or internet is down.
- For each Discovery Companion Meeting, we suggest that you decide ahead of time which one of you will act as facilitator and timekeeper, to guide the pacing of the meeting and ensure that each Companion has adequate time to share, and that you get to all of the components of the Discovery Companions Meeting.
- Have one or both of you read the Opening Prayer aloud as you begin, knowing that this is the prayer of the *Imago Christi* Community for you as well.
- You may choose to add your own prayers for the protection and guidance of the Discovery Companions Meetings.
- Then have the designated facilitator lead the Abiding Prayer Exercise as indicated, as a further preparation of your hearts for this Meeting, and as a means to build the bonds of spiritual community between you as you *together* abide in God with Christ through the Holy Spirit.
- Take just a few minutes to share the fruit of that Abiding Prayer Exercise with each other.
- Share your experience and insights gained from the "Deepening Discovery Exercises" for that Session, as instructed.
- Utilize the Peer-Coaching Principles below to provide each other with the safety and freedom to share whatever the Spirit leads you to share from your experience.
- Encourage one another with "Mutual Support and Prayer," starting with prayer support for the things already experienced and shared in this Session, and then moving on to other prayer requests as appropriate, or needed, and as time allows.
- Close each Discovery Companions Meeting by read aloud together the Closing Prayer provided, followed by your own personal closing prayers for the session.
- Reconfirm the date, time and location of your next Meeting before you end this one.

Peer-Coaching Principles: We want to encourage you as Discovery Companions to maintain a posture of listening to God in and through your Companion's sharing, rather than taking an active role in mentoring, counseling, or teaching each other. The instructions for the "Debrief and Sharing" portion of the Companions Meetings will provide you with guidelines for each Session on your roles as both "speaker" and "listener." Remember:

- Peer-Coaching helping the other person listen to God
- Peer-Coaching is largely an exercise in listening:
    - Listening to the other person
    - Listening to your own thoughts and feelings
    - Listening to God
- We help the other gain insight by *asking questions* that are open ended (rather than giving answers).
- Advice giving or problem solving is usually not helpful
- Feel free to gently encourage each other to follow these guidelines.
- Refer to Coaching Questions (Discovery Workbook v.10e2, p. 56).

Additional Resources are also included at the end of each Session. These are not meant to overburden your Session Preparation, but are suggested resources for your further spiritual growth and enrichment along the themes of that Session. If your Meetings are more than a week apart, you may wish to peruse some of these resources. Otherwise the Additional Resources are meant to help you discern where you will go from here after you have completed all eight sessions of the *Exercises for Discovery Companions*.

Discovery Companions Covenant: "Spiritual Formation happens best in an authentic community of trust, truth and clear expectations." Because these Exercises comprise a journey *together*, we suggest that Discovery Companions *covenant* together before the Lord and each other to complete these *Exercises for Discovery Companions.* In your Opening Session we ask you to commit to the following covenant formula, which is based on portions of the Rule of Life for the Order of *Imago Christi.*

> Having responded to the Spirit's call to personal transformation and intimacy with God in Christ, let us covenant together by the grace of God, as Discovery Companions, to deepen our First Order Calling to love God and to serve Him, that provides the foundation for our Communion with the Trinity, our Community with each other, and our Second Order Callings to love God by loving others in our world.
>
> I dedicate myself to the Lord and by His grace to my Discovery Companion in the context of the *Exercises for Discovery Companions*, as an expression of my love and greater Longing for God, for His glory, the growth of His Kingdom and the beautification of His Bride.
>
> I commit to pray daily for my Discovery Companion, to complete the Exercises to the best of my ability, to attend each of our Discovery Companion meetings, and participate in a spirit of humility and grace.

Our Blessing For
Your Discovery Companion Exercises

May the Lord bless you. May He knit your hearts together in love for one another. As you seek His face, may you be united in truth, encouraging one another to better understand the breadth and depth of His love for you. May the Lord Jesus shower you with His abundant grace and fill you with His perfect peace. To Him be all the glory and praise forever and ever. Amen.

Abiding Prayer for Discovery Companions

All of the Discovery Companion Sessions involve Abiding Prayer Exercises, both for your individual preparation, and for your meetings together with your Companion. When we intentionally and regularly *abide with God* in prayer, just being with God, loving Him and receiving his love, we find we are empowered to discern his presence and voice in the midst of our lives, our relationships and ministry with others. Therefore, rather than treating Abiding Prayer as a separate Session, and since the journey of Abiding Prayer is central to our spiritual formation journey as a whole, we decided to weave Abiding Prayer Exercises into all of the Sessions.

You are free to choose either *Lectio Divina*, Ignatian Prayer, Wordless Prayer, and Contemplation as the focus of the Abiding Prayer Exercises in the Discovery Companions meetings. It is worth repeating our suggestion that you start your Abiding Prayer Exercises, utilizing the approach to prayer that works best for you, for example, *Lectio Divina*, or Ignatian Prayer. After a few days or weeks try to branch out to incorporate approaches that are less familiar to you, Wordless Prayer or Contemplation. In time, you may find yourself moving during a single Abiding Prayer Exercise from a form of active meditation, into more passive forms of prayer. There is no need to rush this process. This is a journey of a lifetime. Like learning any language, we learn Abiding Prayer best by doing and practice, rather than by simply discussing theories or mastering methods. The Lord is by your side, guiding and teaching you. Jump in! You were made in His image for this! The key to Abiding Prayer is *attentiveness* to the Lord, whereby we become receptive to His loving presence, transforming the soul into the image of Christ, so that we relate to the Father in the same way that Jesus did.

Abiding Prayer focuses our on First Order love relationship with God in the first place, as we move more toward listening to God and attending to Him, rather than on talking to God in an otherwise one way conversation. And yet we never really "grow out of" or leave verbal prayer behind. Verbal prayer always remains a necessary and vital part of our relationship with God. He still bids us to "ask, seek and knock," to intercede for others, and simply to cast our cares on Him.

However, if *all* we do is express *ourselves* to God in verbal prayer even with the best language of adoration, confession, thanksgiving and supplication, we still risk remaining in control of the conversation. Prayer can too easily become all about productivity and effectiveness – ours and God's. We slowly realize that our prayer has subtly been focused on bending God to our will, rather bending our will to his. Prayer ends up being another activity, something *we* do, an "it," rather than part of a *relationship*. Our prayer life is all about me, because our relationship with God is all about me. Meanwhile, God patiently waits until we realize that we are not in charge. A realization that comes often through the "failures" and crises that arise, when God refuses to play by our rules and expectations any more. He wants so much *more*!

And there *is* more! There is *always* more. God is always inviting us into more, because the Triune God is the "more" that our hearts truly desire. God wants not only to be Savior, not only Lord, but the Love and the Lover of our life! God has patiently listened to us, stooped to speak our language, condescended to our categories, given us the needed guidance at the critical moments, and blessed our plans. But He wants more *for* us than being obedient soldiers carrying out orders. He longs for us to be his beloved sons and daughters, his friends. And if we will stop trying to second guess what God wants *from* us, we will find that He wants so much more *with* us as well.

What if we stopped just "doing prayer," and intentionally moved in opposite direction of our tendencies to control and manipulate God? What if we just stopped talking? What if we got past the awkward silence, and just sat with Him, and started listening? Listening to God's Word in new ways, and to the movements of the Spirit in our own hearts. We might find that God desires to communicate and commune with us in his language, according to his transcendent categories, to teach us to intuit his heart, and do so continuously, so that everywhere we go we live and minister out of the overflow of his life in us, so everything we put our hands to is blessed with his presence and power in us. Ultimately, God desires us to commune with Him in his Triune Community.

Abiding Prayer is the unique way that we can actively demonstrate our trust in God. The submission of our lives to God is not just a surrender of the *activities* of our lives, but our very beings, our whole self, our *existence* to God in the love of God.

But the ability to slow down and abide with God does not come overnight. It is a habit of the heart that must be developed over time and with time. Abiding Prayer is a journey, the journey of a lifetime, of a life with God, a journey in love that is accomplished by love that transforms us in love, and leads us further into the Love that is God.

Four Movements of Abiding Prayer:

> **Meditation:** Focusing our thoughts on God in the context of Scripture or another object in creation that reflects its Creator. This takes our wandering thoughts and redirects them intentionally to the Lord. *Lectio Divina,* Ignatian Prayer, and Breath Prayer are forms of meditation.

> **Wordless Prayer:** Observing the *thoughts and feelings* that surface in prayer, *without* the response of words, but attentiveness to ourselves in the Lord.

> **Contemplation:** Focusing on God alone. We move from being quiet and attentive to our own souls, to becoming fully attentive to Him, who inhabits our innermost being. We seek His face in silence.

> **Silence:** Prayer without thoughts, words, or mental images – prayer that God brings to us, usually as part of contemplation.
> > (see Discovery Workbook v.10e2, pp. 47-52)

The Four Movements in Practice:

Abiding Prayer need not contain all of these four movements, nor do they necessarily progress in a linear fashion with distinct boundaries. It is enough to "show up" and go as far as you are able, as far as you can let the Lord take you, as far as He knows you are ready to go. We can only offer God our intentional exercises in increasing attentiveness and responsiveness to God in his love. And that is the essence of any spiritual discipline, a method of putting ourselves at God's disposal for Him to transform and grace us as He wills.

Begin with the two forms of Meditation mentioned during Discovery: *Lectio Divina* and Ignatian Prayer. As you become more receptive to abiding with God in prayer, you may experience Contemplation or even Silence come and go in the midst of other movements of Abiding Prayer.

We invite you to explore and experiment with these four movements of prayer in your Abiding Prayer Exercises alone and with your Companion. Offer these movements of Abiding Prayer along with your very selves to God to use them to transform you in his love, in his way and in his perfect time.

Lectio Divina

Read a short passage of Scripture, slowly and repetitively, preferably out loud in this form of Meditation called "divine reading." Pay attention to what the Lord seems to be highlighting, for us personally, from the text. Allow it to penetrate deep into our souls. Listen for God to communicate with you through the words and simply in the context of his Word.

Practical Suggestions	**Comments**
Choose a Bible Passage	Keep it short, a single Gospel passage or paragraph, rather than a whole chapter.
Settle in silence	Choose a comfortable posture in a place without distractions.
Center yourself	Breath Prayer can be helpful to redirect the attention of our minds, and emotions from ourselves to the Lord. Take a word or phrase that Holy Spirit highlighted in your reading, as a "Breath Prayer," repeating the word or phrase over and over in harmony with your breathing until you return to a place of quiet attentiveness where can continue to be attentive to the Lord and how He may guide you.
Become attentive to the Lord's guidance	Pay attention to what the Spirit seems to highlight. What seems to jump off the page?
Read slowly and repetitively.	Read the text slowly three times, interspersed with silence. Keep your mind open to whatever impressions or aspects of the text that seems to speak to you in your current circumstances.
Reflect in Silence	After the readings, be still with God for about five minutes at first, and then longer with practice. Give the Lord opportunity to guide your reflection, and possibly take you into Wordless Prayer, Contemplation, or Silence.
Dealing with Distractions	As your mind starts to wander, don't get agitated; return to the passage, or a portion of the passage and read it again. It may be helpful to use the highlighted passage as a Breath Prayer, and then let the Breath Prayer fade as your mind and emotions are centered again.
Journal	You may also choose to Journal your experience.

Ignatian Prayer

Use your imagination in prayer to vividly experience a Biblical story. As we engage God's Word with our imagination, the Lord speaks not only to our understanding, but inspires our senses and touches our hearts.

Practical Suggestions	Comments
Choose a Text	Biblical narratives and Gospel passages fit best
Use your imagination to "be there"	Imaginatively place yourself in the story as one of the characters or an observant bystander. Let the scene come alive. See it, feel it, smell it.
Listen to yourself and God	Notice what it is in the story that attracts your attention. Observe your responsive thoughts and feelings to that aspect of the story. What do your responses tell you about yourself? What might God be saying to you in your responses?
Be still with Him	Become quiet and be attentive to God's presence with you. Be receptive to His leading. Give the Lord opportunity to guide, take you into Wordless Prayer, Contemplation, or Silence.
Dealing with Distractions	When your mind starts to wander, don't react; gently return to your imaging of the passage, or read it again.
Respond to Him	Respond or follow as He leads. Interact with the Lord conversationally. Allow the Holy Spirit to pray within you. The scene in our imagination may go beyond the words of the text, because his presence is very real.
Reflect	You may also choose to journal your experience.

Wordless Prayer

Observe and offer the thoughts and emotions that surface in our hearts and minds during a prayer time, but without formulating a mental or verbal response. We intentionally refrain from reciting lists and instructions to God of what to do and how to do it. In Wordless Prayer we allow God to surface the thoughts, emotions, scenes and people that are part of our lives, and gently turn the attention of our hearts towards God in and through them.

Practical Suggestions:

- You may begin with a short Meditation, or you may start with Wordless Prayer as a way to discern where God may want to take the discussion.
- Become still and attentive to yourself, your body, your thoughts, and your emotions in the context of God presence. Assume that He is a part of what comes to mind.
- Do not try to control your thoughts, but simply observe. If you notice that you have begun to follow the thoughts, such as planning some coming event, simply resume to your focus on the Lord.
- Allow God to interact with your thoughts and feelings, without verbalizing prayers; allow the Holy Spirit to pray within you. Watch for whatever agenda the Lord might be setting for more focused prayer.

Comments:

- We actively remain passively attentive to what is going on in our heart and mind, without engaging, discussing, interpreting or interrupting it with words.
- We do not attempt to take control and talk to God about a particular subject. But we observe the responses of our thoughts and emotions, and listen to what God might be saying to us as this "parade" of experiences flows by.
- Wordless Prayer can feel like a "creative mind-wandering." It is creative because God is interacting within us in the process.
- When the review is over, lift the people or concerns before the Lord, letting His loving presence embrace them. It may be helpful to choose a gesture, whether in your imagination and/or with your body, that symbolizes your response an interaction with the Lord. For example: hold them in your heart; lift them up; place them in His hands; let his light or warmth shine on them).
- In closing you may now use language to express your response to God in intercession, questions, worship, as your feel led. You may want to ask Jesus, our High Priest and Intercessor, how He might be praying for you right now? Give it voice. Speak out his prayers with Him.

Contemplation

Maintain your focus on God alone. We move from being quiet and attentive to ourselves, to becoming more fully attentive to Him who inhabits our innermost being.

Practical Suggestions:

- Find a comfortable posture and quiet place alone. Reclining isn't usually helpful; it often leads to falling asleep.
- Take some time initially to tell God what is on your mind, simply and quickly so that you become free to simply be present with Him.
- You may begin with a brief Scripture, or a Breath Prayer to help you Still your mind and focus on God. "Call upon the Name of the Lord" (Jesus, Father, Abba, Lord) to direct your heart and mind.
- If helpful use an object, or a symbol, a cross, a candle, a picture of Christ as a visual aid to focus your attention on Him, but then slowly let go of the aid and allow your focus to transcend any thing but Him.
- Be still. Seek God's face. Feel, "listen to," and be aware of God. Behold God with continued attention, but without words, thoughts, or mental images. Be present to Him. Attend to God intentionally.
- Don't chase "lights" or respond to attacks.
- Lights: Giving attention to insights rather than to the Lord Himself.
- Attacks: Condemnation, guilt the Enemy uses to turn our attention off of God and back onto ourselves.
- Seek God's Face, but don't strain. Contemplation is not like mountain climbing, trying to get to somewhere else. God lives within us, present, loving us, so we simply abide in Him. We are spreading our wings to catch the updrafts of the winds of the Spirit, simply enjoying communion with God in his loving presence.
- Close with The Lord's Prayer, a Psalm, a verbal or mental prayer.
- Journal your experience

Comments:

- Remember Contemplation is something that God does for us.
- This is the God-intended direction, focus and destiny of our journey of prayer (see 1John 3:2).
- Don't worry, if this seems beyond you. Focus your attention on other more meditative forms of prayer and the Lord will invite you into Contemplation in his good time.

Silence

Communion with God that ultimately transcends our human words or categories, reflecting the transcendent nature of God. This is where we no longer have to hold our attention on God; He is holding us.

Practical Suggestions:

- God can gift us with silence at any place in Abiding Prayer, but we most often experience it in the midst of contemplation.
- Move toward contemplation in the ways suggested above in complete surrender to the Lord's presence and love.
- Be still
- Surrender yourself, your needs and desires to Jesus as your Good Shepherd
- As much as possible, let love of God be your motivation for abiding with Him.
- Try not to look for signs of communing silence; we usually notice that it has happened when it is over.
- Continue in contemplation until the Lord releases you.
- Close your contemplative time as described above

Comments:

- This spiritual communion with God feels like the momentary "silences" of our mind and body, given by God within contemplative prayer.
- This spiritual silence is a gift of grace.
- We cannot produce this Silence of ourselves, or control it.
- We can, however, diligently seek to increase our receptivity to this grace by predisposing ourselves to it through Contemplation.

Considerations for Your Journey of Abiding Prayer

Be patient with yourself. Most of us have experienced becoming quiet and still while walking in the woods, or sitting on the beach. We may sort of just "feel into it" while visiting some very special place, but have no idea how to enter into it when back home in the busyness and pressures of everyday life.

The first efforts of seeking Abiding Prayer may seem like they are filled with futile attempts to "shush" our frantically distracted minds that seem terrified of being ignored. It may seem impossible, but everything is possible with God. Follow your Longing and his! Keep at it. Over time, you will develop habits and rhythms that will become second nature. You will begin to catch brief moments of quiet, then longer moments, and then occasional and more frequent stretches of silence, usually after years of practice along this journey of Abiding Prayer.

Remember: the key to Abiding Prayer is *attentiveness* to the Lord, whereby we become more receptive to His loving presence, transforming the soul into the image of Christ, so that we relate to the Father in the same way that Jesus did.

This is a journey of love into love. The primary goal is to attend to God, be with God in his love, according to our First Order Calling. You will experience that relational focus with God in love with the help of Scripture passages at first, but more and more as you surrender your self to God in prayer, you will experience the "more" that God has, and is, for you.

You are a beloved child of God. Seek and you shall find. Knock and it shall be opened to you. He is already at the door with dinner in His hands.

Additional Resources: (see. p. 6)

- M. Robert Mulholland, Jr. "Spiritual Disciplines" in *An Invitation to a Journey: A Roadmap for the Spiritual Journey.*

- Richard Foster, *Prayer.*

- William Shannon, *Silence on Fire.*

Opening Session:
Companions in Discovery

1. Before you begin:

    - Arrange the date, time, location and conferencing venue for this Opening Session with your Discovery Companion.
    - Review all of the Introductory Material in this guide and seek clarity on any questions you may have for the *Exercises for Discovery Companions*.
    - Allow 1-1/2 to 2 hours for this session.
    - The Goal for this Session is to get acquainted with each other and the process designed for you here in the *Exercises for Discovery Companions*.
    - Bring: your Timeline, Discovery Manual, Journal, and Bible.

2. Opening Prayer: Choose one person to read the following prayer, followed by your own personal prayers for this session and series of Exercises.

    O Lord, we bless You for constantly inviting us into deeper intimacy with you through the Lord Jesus Christ, in the fellowship of the Holy Spirit. We thank You for bringing us together for this season as Discovery Companions.

    Guide each of us as we seek You through these Exercises, and knit us more closely together as Companions in Your Spirit through this experience, as we meet, and share, and support, and pray for one another on their journey deeper into Your love.

3. Abiding Prayer Exercise: Psalm 46 (10-15 minutes)

    Have the other companion both read the text aloud (3x) and keep track of time. Afterwards, sit with God in silence for 1-2 minutes.

We invite you to briefly share the following (about 5 minutes each).

- Did any specific words or images from the text—or in response to the text—seem to speak to you?
- What did you experience?
- What did you feel?
- What was your physical, emotional and/or spiritual response?
- In what ways do you think you may have experienced Jesus?

4. Orientation to the Exercises for Discovery Companions:
   - Introductions: introduce yourselves to each other.
   - How did the Companions find each other?
   - Sharing your hopes and expectations: What do you want from these sessions?
   - Review the components and process in the Introductory Materials.
   - Review the "Abiding Prayer Exercises" and "Deepening Discovery Exercise" for Session 1 to clarify the process.
   - Do you have any questions about the process?
   - Encourage the Discovery Companions to make a Covenant commitment to the Lord and each other for the duration of these Exercises (see p. 7).

     Having responded to the Spirit's call to personal transformation and intimacy with God in Christ, let us covenant together by the grace of God, as Discovery Companions, to deepen our First Order Calling to love God and to serve Him, that provides the foundation for our Communion with the Trinity, our Community with each other, and our Second Order Callings to love God by loving others in our world.

     I dedicate myself to the Lord and by His grace to my Discovery Companion in the context of the *Exercises for Discovery Companions*, as an expression of my love and greater Longing for God, for His glory, the growth of His Kingdom and the beautification of His Bride.

     I commit to pray daily for my Discovery Companion, to complete the Exercises to the best of my ability, to attend each of our Discovery Companion meetings, and participate in a spirit of humility and grace.

5. Mutual Support, Sharing & Prayer:

- Pray for each other as Discovery Companions, for any current prayer requests.

- Closing Prayer: conclude with your own personal prayers for completing these Exercises together.

- Pronounce a Blessing on each other as you begin these Exercises for Discovery Companions (in unison):

  May the Lord bless you. May He knit our hearts together in love for one another. As we seek His face, may we be united in truth, encouraging one another to better understand the breadth and depth of His love for us. May the Lord Jesus shower us with His abundant grace and fill us with His perfect peace. To Him be all the glory and praise forever and ever. Amen.

- Confirm your next two sessions (time/location).

- **Hint: Look ahead at the second Exercise in Session 3 on "Spiritual Longing" (p. 36), and plan ahead to schedule your Beauty Project.**

Session 1: Spiritual Timeline – Telling Your Story

SESSION PREPARATION

Goals:

- To gain deeper insights into your timeline
- To build community through the sharing of timelines
- To hear and affirm each other's unique journey
- To establish an environment of trust and acceptance

Abiding Prayer Exercises (refer to the instructions on Abiding Prayer on pp. 4, 8-16)

1. Deuteronomy 8:2-5
2. Psalm 139:1-18
3. Luke 5:1-10
4. Luke 24:13-35
5. Ephesians 2:1-10

Deepening Discovery Exercises: (refer to the instructions on pp. 4-5)

1.   Review the details, events, and insights of your Timeline and add any more "Sticky Notes" and Insights that come to mind. Spend some focused time in reflection over each Chapter or Season of your Timeline, and write down your additions:
  - Key Chapter Insights: lessons and insights that the Lord revealed to you through specific events and seasons of your life.
  - Key Timeline Insights: lessons and insights about your spiritual life as you look at your Timeline as a whole. What is God after? What is He doing over the course of your life? What is life with God all about?

2.   Journal about your Timeline in light of Deuteronomy 8:2-5. Pick two or three of the following questions that resonate with you most.

- How has the Lord "humbled" you along your Timeline? (v. 2a).
- How has the Lord "tested what was in your heart" along your journey? (v. 2b).
- What lessons did the Lord's humbling teach you? (v. 3).
- In what ways did the Lord specifically provide for you, so that you could continue on this journey of spiritual discovery? How have you noticed that this Timeline exercise has increased your faith to trust God for what He is doing in the moment? (v. 4).
- In what ways can you see the Lord's discipline at work in your life? (v. 5a).
- How well have you been able to see the Lord's "discipline" as an expression of God's love for you along this journey? (v. 5b, see also Hebrews 12:5-11).
- Thank the Lord for this journey, and His faithfulness along this journey to lead you into deeper intimacy with Him.

3. Review Peer-Coaching principles: (see p. 6)

- Peer-Coaching helping the other person listen to God

- Peer-Coaching is largely an exercise in listening:

  - Listening to the other person

  - Listening to your own thoughts and feelings

  - Listening to God

- We help the other gain insight by *asking questions* that are open ended (rather than giving answers).

- Advice giving or problem solving is usually not helpful

- Feel free to gently encourage each other to follow these guidelines.

- Refer to Coaching Questions (Discovery Workbook v.10e2, p. 56).

COMPANIONS MEETING FOR SESSION 1:

1. Before you meet:

    ●   Complete the "Abiding Prayer Exercises" and "Deepening
        Discovery Exercises" with enough time for reflection prior to
        meeting.
    ●   Allow 1-1/2 to 2 hours for this session.
    ●   Review the goals for this session.
    ●   Bring: Timeline, Discovery Manual, Discovery Event Pre-work,
        your journal for these Exercises, Bible, and your personal
        calendar. (We strongly recommend scheduling at least two
        sessions ahead.)

2. Opening Prayer: Please read aloud together, followed by your own
    personal prayers for this session.

> O Lord of our hearts, and Lord of the ages, You who have
> numbered our days, ordered our paths and chosen us in Christ
> before the foundation of the world, spark our memories and open
> our hearts to Your presence and activity in our lives. You have
> brought us together now to journey as spiritual companions for
> this season. Help us be good listeners to each other's heart for
> You, and to Your heart for each one of us. Guide our
> conversation by Your Spirit and form our hearts in the image of
> the Lord Jesus. Amen.

3. Abiding Prayer Exercise: Deuteronomy 8:2-5 (10-15 minutes) (see. p. 5)

   Choose one person to both read the text aloud (3x) and keep track of time. Afterwards, sit with God in silence for 1-2 minutes.

   We invite you to briefly share the following (about 5 minutes each).

   - Did any specific words or images from the text—or in response to the text—seem to speak to you?
   - What did you experience?
   - What did you feel?
   - What was your physical, emotional and/or spiritual response?
   - In what ways do you think you may have experienced Jesus?

4. Debrief: Timeline Sharing (40-60 minutes)

   - Give each Companion 20-30 minutes for each person to summarize his or her Timeline, in order to provide your Discovery Companion with significant background information to understand your journey.

   - As the speaker, focus your sharing on:
     o What were the major challenges to your spiritual growth?
     o What were some of the most consistent inspirations for your spiritual growth?
     o What were some key insights?
     o How did God touch you as you reviewed your Timeline in the Deepening Discovery Exercises?

   - As the listener:
     o Only ask clarifying questions at this point.
     o What can you affirm in the speaker's story?

5.   Mutual Support, Sharing & Prayer: (30 minutes)

    a. Pray for one another in the joys and struggles related to this
session and for any current prayer requests.

    b. Closing Prayer: Please read aloud together, followed by your
own personal closing prayers for this session.

Lord, we are standing on holy ground for the stories of our
Timelines recount the many ways that You have revealed
Yourself in our lives. We bow before Your infinite mercy and
patience with us. We marvel at the persistence with which You
pursue us. Lord, strengthen us in our inner beings for the journey
ahead into deeper intimacy with You, as You continue to reveal
Your will, Your heart, Your very Self to us, we pray to You,
Father, Son and Holy Spirit. Amen.

    c. Confirm the next two sessions (time/location).

Additional Resources:

- Janet O. Hagberg and Robert A. Guelich, *The Critical Journey: Stages in the Life of Faith.*

- Sibyl Towner and Sharon Swing, *Listen to My Life: Maps for Recognizing and Responding to God in My Story.*

- David G. Benner, *The Gift of Being Yourself.*

- R. Thomas Ashbrook, *Mansions of the Heart*, Jossey-Bass, 2009.

Session 2: Spiritual Timeline – Views of God

SESSION PREPARATION

Goals:

- To gain deeper insights into how you viewed and related to God in the past
- To build community through the sharing of Timelines
- To continue to build a safe, peer relationship

Abiding Prayer Exercises: (refer to the instructions on Abiding Prayer on pp. 4, 8-16)

1. Psalm 145
2. 2 Samuel 22:2-4
3. John 10:1-18
4. Philippians 2:5-11
5. John 14:25-30

Deepening Discovery Exercises: (see pp. 4-5)

1. Revisit your Timeline with this question: What has been your experiential View of God over time?
    - First, pray and ask the Spirit to clarify how you viewed and related to God.
    - Next, use the "Views of God" sheet on the next page that lists Scriptural references for various "Views of God." **Which of the following Views of God have been connected to the various events of your life?** Make notes on this sheet.
    - Add or move green Sticky Notes to your Timeline to mark the shifts in your operational view of God over time.
    - Additional Key Timeline Insights: How did your views of God change or strengthen in your journey? How is God inviting you to know Him now? Be ready to recount to your companion a recent experience, which demonstrates your current View of God.
    - Close this time with the Lord with a short time of worship and thanksgiving.

Views of God Exercise

God as:	Reference	Your Life Event:	Opposite view
Personal Creator	Psalm 139:13		Impersonal Life Force
Protective Judge	Psalm 96:13		Unjust Judge
Good Shepherd	Isaiah 40:11		Wolf
Helper	Psalm 54:4		Uninvolved
King	Psalm 47		Vending Machine
Father	Luke 11:13		Abuser
Provider	Philippians 4:19		Withholder
Loving Husband	Isaiah 54:5		Fickle Paramour
Warrior	Exodus 15:3		Passive
Lord	Jeremiah 22:37		Good Teacher
Savior	Luke 19:10		Disinterested
Friend	John 15:15		Enemy
Deliverer	Psalm 18:2		Punisher
Servant	Matthew 20:28		Abusive Overlord
Healer	Psalm 30:2		Inflictor of Pain
Almighty	Revelation 1:8		Impotent
Reward	Genesis 15:1		Burden

2. Additional optional exercises related to your Timeline:

- Journal 3-5 personal encounters with God.
- Sketch a symbol or write key words that represent how you experienced God in any one of the encounters above.

3. Review Peer-Coaching principles: (see p. 6)

- Peer-Coaching helping the other person listen to God
- Peer-Coaching is largely an exercise in listening:
    - Listening to the other person
    - Listening to your own thoughts and feelings
    - Listening to God
- We help the other gain insight by *asking questions* that are open ended (rather than giving answers).
- Advice giving or problem solving is usually not helpful
- Feel free to gently encourage each other to follow these guidelines.
- Refer to Coaching Questions (Discovery Workbook v.10e2, p. 56).

COMPANIONS MEETING FOR SESSION 2:

1. Before you meet:

    - Complete the Abiding Prayer and Deepening Discovery Exercises with enough time for reflection prior to meeting.
    - Allow 1-1/2 to 2 hours for this session.
    - Review the goals for this session.
    - Bring: Discovery Manual, Timeline, your journal for these exercises, Bible, and your personal Calendar.

2. Opening Prayer: Please read aloud together, followed by your own personal prayers for this session.

    > O Lord, You invite us into an ever-deepening relationship—to know You more and to love You better every day. We release to You the misconceptions we have carried concerning who we believed You to be. We thank You for leading us into growing awareness of who You are. As we share our hearts regarding our new insights with one another as spiritual companions, help us to be good listeners to each other's heart for You, and to Your heart for each one of us. Guide our conversation by Your Spirit and form our hearts in the image of the Lord Jesus. Amen.

3. Abiding Prayer Exercise: Psalm 23 (10-15 minutes)

    Choose one person to both read the text aloud (3x) as an Ignatian, imaginative exercise, and to keep track of time; it may not be the same as the time-keeper for the Session. Afterwards, sit quietly with God in imaginative silence for 1-2 minutes.

    Briefly share the following (about 5 minutes each).

    - Did any specific words or images from the text—or in response to the text—seem to speak to you?
    - What did you experience?
    - What did you feel?
    - What was your physical, emotional and/or spiritual response?
    - In what ways do you think you may have experienced Jesus?

4.   Sharing Insights: (40-60 minutes)

    i.   Give each Companion 30-40 minutes to share their insights from examining their Views of God.

    ii.   Focus sharing on:
- Any changes made on the Timeline
- Which Views of God remained consistent for long periods of time or strengthened or radically changed?
- What life events have had the greatest impact on changing your views? How did this new understanding affect the subsequent events?
- How did God touch you through your Abiding Prayer and Deepening Discovery Exercises?
- Share your current View of God.

5.   Mutual Support, Sharing & Prayer: (30 minutes)

- Pray for one another in the joys and struggles related to this session and for any current prayer requests.
- Closing Scripture: choose a Companion to read Jeremiah 9:23-24 aloud:

> Thus says the LORD: 'Let not the wise man boast in his wisdom, let not the mighty man boast in his might, let not the rich man boast in his riches, but let him who boasts boast in this, that He understands and knows Me, that I am the LORD who practices steadfast love, justice, and righteousness in the earth.' 'For in these things I delight,' declares the LORD.

- Closing prayer: Please read aloud together, followed by your own personal closing prayers for this session.

  > Lord, we thank You for inviting us into the great blessing of knowing You, being drawn ever deeper into the 'fullness of Christ' by gaining a better understanding of who You are. May this understanding lead us into wisdom and strength in following You into deeper intimacy with the Father, as Your disciples. Amen.

- Confirm the next two sessions (time/location).

Additional Resources:

- Brennan Manning, *Abba's Child.*
- J.B. Phillips, *Your God is Too Small*

Session 3: Spiritual Longing

SESSION PREPARATION

Goals:

- To learn to see and hear what your heart longs for in your relationship with God and to know His heart's Longing to fulfill it.
- To practice holding your Longing in your heart and abiding with God in it.
- To recognize how the Spirit's intercession works within you to refine (or redefine) your Longing
- To encourage and support one another in discovering and pursuing the Longing that the Lord has hidden in your hearts.

Abiding Prayer Exercises:

1. Psalm 63:1-5 (Complete with Exercise 1 below.)
2. Psalm 27:4 (Complete with Exercise 2 below.)
3. Psalm 42
4. Isaiah 26:7-9
5. Romans 8:14-23

Deepening Discovery Exercises:

Exercise 1: Share your Longing statement with the Lord. (Allow 60 minutes)

- Review the section on Longing in the *Discovering Your Spiritual Formation Journey* (15 min).
- Find a quiet place to sit and pray without distractions. Imagine yourself in your Longing picture. Hold your Longing picture in your mind and ask the Holy Spirit to show you where it might be refined to express His Longing for you.
- Ask the Spirit to search your picture of your heart's Longing and refine, or redefine, how it expresses God's gracious desire for your fellowship.

- Abiding Prayer Exercise: Psalm 63:1-5 (30 min)
  - Read the text slowly 3x.
  - What verse or image stood out to you?
  - Insert your Longing image into that the verse that stood out to you from Psalm 63:1-5.

Examples of Longing images inserted in italics below:

> *As a tree beside a river,* my soul thirsts for You.

> *As a babe in her Father's hands*, my flesh yearns for You.

> My God, my God, *as a sail seeks the wind*, I shall seek You earnestly.

> My soul is satisfied *as we walk together.*

  - Use your combined image as a gentle Breath Prayer to enter into a place of stillness, abiding with the Lord.
  - Sit in this stillness for 10 minutes, returning to the Breath Prayer as you become distracted.

Option 1: Journal your experience:

- What did you experience?
- Reflect on what transpired. Did the Lord do anything with your picture? If so, what?
- How did that feel to you? What emotional response to the Lord did you experience?
- What did you receive from the Lord?

Option 2: Draw your experience.

- Draw symbolic representation of the Spirit's intercession for your Longing.

- Using crayons, colored pencils or markers to draw any impressions of scenes, images, or symbols that represent your Longing. If a word, then write it down as word art.
- What feelings are related to what you have drawn? What feelings were further evoked by drawing your Longing?
- What blessing did you receive from the Lord?

Exercise 2: Beauty Project

When we practice paying more attention to God, we are more likely to find our Longing for God reflected in the beauty of nature and art.

- Choose an activity from this following list and watch for an expression of your Longing, then with the experience still fresh, proceed to the Abiding Prayer Exercise.
  - o Watch a movie
  - o Go to an art gallery
  - o Take a walk in nature
  - o Take an architectural walking tour
  - o Listen to a symphony
  - o Watch and opera
  - o Watch a sunset
  - o Other experience of beauty
- Abiding Prayer Exercise: Psalm 27:4
- Journal your thoughts, feelings and insights from your prayer time.
  - o How did your Longing find expression, perhaps new expression through this Exercise?
  - o How did you experience the Lord revealing His Longing to you?
  - o What insights did you gain about yourself or the Lord?
  - o What did you long for?
  - o How did this experience interact with your Longing Statement?

Exercise 3: Revise your Longing Statement in light of these Exercises.

- Consider: Can you see it? Feel it? Does it engage your passion to pursue it?
- Think of one other person in addition to your Companion, with whom you could share your Longing Statement over the next week.

COMPANIONS MEETING FOR SESSION 3:

1.   Before you meet:

- Complete the Abiding Prayer and Deepening Discovery Exercises with enough time for reflection prior to meeting.
- Allow 1-1/2 to 2 hours for this session.
- Review the goals for this session.
- Bring: Discovery Manual, Timeline, your journal for these exercises, Bible, and your personal calendar.

2.   Opening Prayer: Please read aloud together, followed by your own personal prayers for this session.

> *He has made everything beautiful in its own time. He has also set eternity in the human heart, yet no one can fathom what God has done from beginning to end. (Ecclesiastes 3:11)*

> O God, we long for You with our whole hearts, or at least we long to long for You that way. Help us to get in touch with that deep Longing that You have placed deep within our souls. Help us to trust the stirrings within us as being from You. Give us an image that can gently ease us back into the deep desires of our hearts for relationship with You, especially when we find our hearts wandering from You, or we find ourselves mindlessly moving through our days without awareness of Your presence. Grant us words that articulate for ourselves, if no one else, what we desire in a relationship with You. Thank You for this good gift and thank You for the already present Longing You have for relationship with us. Amen.

3.   Abiding Prayer Exercise: Psalm 63:1-5 (10-15 minutes)

Choose one person to both read the text aloud (3x) and keep track of time. Afterwards, sit with God in silence for 1-2 minutes.

We invite you to briefly share the following (about 5 minutes each).

- Did any specific words or images from the text—or in response to the text—seem to speak to you?
- What did you experience?
- What did you feel?
- What was your physical, emotional and/or spiritual response?
- In what ways do you think you may have experienced Jesus?

4.   Longing Sharing (40-60 minutes):

- Have each Companion simply name their Longing image without explanation. Sit with those images for a minute.
- Have each Companion read their current Longing Statement, such as it is, understanding that it is a work-in-progress, and that it is our best understanding to date.
- Share key reflections from the Deepening Discovery Exercises, focusing sharing particularly on the emotions and feelings connected with your Longing image.
- As a listener, please be careful to not critique, but only to ask questions for clarification.

5.   Mutual Support, Sharing & Prayer

- Pray for each other, that your Longing Statements would become more and more of a reality in your relationships with God and for any current prayer requests.

- Closing Prayer: Please read aloud together, followed by your own personal closing prayers for this session.

  God, our loving Heavenly Father, bring our Longings for You to greater and greater reality. Usher us into Your presence on a regular basis, where we become more and more aware of just how deeply You long for relationship with us. Help us not to shy away from the closeness with which You wish to hold us. Draw us to Yourself this day. We pray in the name of the Father, Son, and Holy Spirit. Amen.

- Confirm the next two sessions (time/location).

Additional Resources:

- C. S. Lewis, *The Great Divorce.* This fantastic journey explores many angles on our hindrances to living in love with God, but also displays amazing images of the delight and fulfillment of life in and with God. The same themes lie behind *The Space Trilogy* and more deeply behind *The Chronicles of Narnia.*
- A. W. Tozer, *The Pursuit of God.*
- William of St.-Thierry, "On Contemplating God – a prelude" in Bernard of Clairvaux. *The Love of God and Spiritual Friendship.* ed. James Houston. Portland, Oregon: Multnomah Press, 1983. pp. 111-113.
- Juan de la Cruz, *Living Flame of Love.* A more challenging text from the middle ages unpacks the poetic verses of the soul kindled by the love of God.

Session 4: Hindrances to Longing

SESSION PREPARATION

Goals:

- To re-examine our blocks to intimacy with God in the context of His love for us expressed in our Longing Statement and image.
- To gain deeper insights into the various sources of the Blocks to living into our Longings.
- To build community through sharing the Hindrances to our Longing.
- To encourage each other to address our Blocks and forgive out of a renewed sense of God's desire for greater intimacy with us.
- To take the next, bold step towards healing, while recognizing that true healing is complex, rarely quick, seldom easy, but rewarding in the end.

An Important Note before you begin:

If you find yourself unable to do the following Abiding Prayer Exercises, please feel free to only do these Exercises to the extent you are able.

If, however you are dealing with *major life traumas*, you may find you are in so much pain that the Deepening Discovery Exercises only intensify your pain, causing you to be overwrought with anger at God, or reduced to tears, convinced that God could never love you, then please skip the rest of these Exercises and simply refer to the notes below "For your additional consideration" (p. 40), the NOTE in the Preparation for the Session (p. 41), and the "Additional Resources" listed at the end (p. 44).

Some of our Blocks and Wounds may feel too big or may run too deep for us to bring to full resolution through the process we have outlined here. However, each time we come to the Lord with our needs, He moves us a step further in healing. But if you are able, perhaps it is just enough to name the wound before God and one other witness and then seek to take just another step towards healing. Healing's greatest deterrents are secrecy, silence, and judgment, so perhaps just verbalizing the problem without sharing any details to your Companion might be a great next step. Very often we have to accept that *healing takes time.* Yet, *as we allow Him,* God keeps us moving toward healing and the experience of our

Longing. Our goal in the Exercises for this Session should be to take the next step towards healing.

Abiding Prayer Exercises

1. Matthew 11:28-30
2. Luke 15:17-24
3. 1 John 4:15-18
4. Romans 8:35-39
5. Genesis 16:6-14 (see also 21:8-21)

Deepening Discovery Exercises:

1. Complete this exercise some time after you have done the first two Abiding Prayer Exercises in preparation for this Session. Take the Block or Wound that you would like to address in this session to your place of Longing with Jesus in the following way
   - Spend some time reading your Longing Statement, and then picturing your Longing image as vividly as you can, notice:
     - What is the metaphor of your relationship with God?
     - Where are you in the image? What are you doing? What do you feel?
     - Where is God in the image? How do you feel towards Him?
   - Get as comfortable with Jesus in your Longing image as you can, and then:
     - Bring your Block or Wound into this picture of love with God by telling Him about your Block or Wound, or showing Him some symbolic representation of it.
     - How do you feel about doing that?
     - How does God react? How does He express His love for you?
     - Ask Him about your Block or Wound. What does He say about it?
       What does He want you to do with it at this point?
     - How do you want to respond to Him?

- Journal about this experience, just describing or recording it first, then feel free to process it further in your journal.
- What is God's invitation to you regarding your Block or Wound?

2. Spend some intentional time reflecting on the groupings and patterns of the "Pink Notes" on your Timeline in light of the following statements:

Blocks to intimacy are the beliefs, the fears, and the lies we allow to keep us from accepting, trusting, and embracing God's life-giving love. At heart, They are often related to our feelings of unworthiness and inferiority, or to our fear of punishment or rejection.

Spiritual Wounds come from the injustices or abuses (done by us or others) that we have internalized, or allowed to define us, that reinforce our Blocks to intimacy. Are there more "Pink Notes" that you need to add to your Timeline?

- How would you describe the evolution of your Block in your Timeline from its source(s) to its various symptoms.
- In what ways can you see that your Block is related to a view of God that is less than loving?
- How does the relational nature of your Longing image relate to the source of your Block?

3. Spend some time reading your Longing Statement and then picture your Longing image as vividly as you can. As you continue your prayerful imagining:

- Notice which of the following personal needs that Jesus fulfills in your Longing image is the most important to you:

    o   I am seen and heard.
    o   I am a person of worth, who matters to God.
    o   I am accepted for who I am.
    o   I am God's beloved.
    o   Other? _____

- Imagine the Lord present in your Longing, speaking forgiveness from the Cross (see Luke 23:34). To whom in your Timeline is He speaking?
- Imagine yourself extending forgiveness with Christ from this place of Longing. Towards whom is your forgiveness directed?
- What is the Lord's invitation to you? How do you want to respond to Him? (Refer to the prayer in your Discovery Workbook, v. 10e2, p. 44 bottom).

For your additional consideration:

As you work with Blocks, you may find a few common indications that you need more support than a Discovery Companion can provide. Working through and seeking the healing of "Blocks" can "stir-up" significant issues. Here are five warning signs that may indicate (if you have 1 or more), it is time to seek the help of a trusted advisor (Pastoral Counselor, Healing Prayer Team, Psychologist, or Psychiatrist):

- **Sleep**: Irregular sleeping patterns.
- **Food**: Inability to eat regularly. Or binge, purging, or bulimic eating.
- **Isolation**: shutting down and avoiding any outside contact with people.
- **Addictive behavior**: excessive alcohol use, drugs, gambling, pornography, or impulse buying.
- **Emotional**: Overwhelming feelings of depression with thoughts of wanting to hurt yourself.

Please keep these warning signs in mind as you share your experiences during the session with your Companion. Know that the listening heart of a spiritual companion in communion with the Holy Spirit is a powerful combination for your healing. In this spiritual community, we find the grace to surrender our Blocks and to receive and extend forgiveness.

COMPANIONS MEETING FOR SESSION 4:

1. Before you meet:

- Complete the Abiding Prayer and Deepening the Discovery Exercises with enough time for reflection prior to meeting. Highlight the points you particularly want to share with your Discovery Companion.
- Allow 1-1/2 to 2 hours for this session.
- Review the Goals for this session.
- Bring: Timeline, Discovery Manual, Journal, Bible, and Calendar (for scheduling your next session).

NOTE:

- If *you* were unable to complete the Exercises for this Session, because of the depth of spiritual wounding, please feel free to participate in this Session only on the level you are comfortable, and seek the prayer and encouragement of your Discovery Companion. Perhaps you can find the courage in this context to name the Wound before God and your Companion, and then commit to taking the next bold step towards healing.

- If *your Companion* was unable to complete the Exercises for this Session, please be gentle, and overly gracious in the support your Companion's ongoing healing. Probably at best in this context, all we can do is provide our Companions with a safe place in which to name the Wound before God and one other witness and then with empathy support your Companion in seeking the next bold step towards healing.

2. Opening Prayer: Please read aloud together, followed by your own personal prayers for this session.

> Lord Jesus, You came to proclaim freedom for the prisoners and recovery of sight for the blind, to set the oppressed free. Lord, we admit that we have been captive to lies that say You don't love us, and we can't trust Your love. We have been blindly attempting to fulfill the deepest desires of our souls apart from You, running away from You, who are our only hope. We need You to open our eyes, to open our hearts, and free us from the oppression of our Blocks to intimacy with You and others. Help us forgive, as You forgive. Help us forgive ourselves, even as You have forgiven us.
>
> Help us to walk in the glorious freedom of the children of God, and trust You to carry us through anything in Your love, for nothing, no thing, can separate us from the love of God that is in Christ Jesus, our Lord, together with the Holy Spirit. Amen.

3. Abiding Prayer Exercise: Romans 8:35-39 (10-15 minutes).

> Choose one person to both read the text aloud (3x) and keep track of time. Afterwards, sit with God in silence for 1-2 minutes. We invite you to briefly share the following (about 5 minutes each).

- Did any specific words or images from the text—or in response to the text—seem to speak to you?
- What did you experience?
- What did you feel? (What was your physical, emotional and/or spiritual response?)
- In what ways do you think you may have experienced Jesus?

4. Debrief & Sharing (40-60 minutes)

- Give each Companion 20-30 minutes to name and, as possible, summarize their reflections on the Hindrances to their Longing.
- As the speaker, focus your sharing on:
  - o The history and development of Blocks and Wounds in your Timeline that have continuously interfered with experiencing your Longing for deeper relationship with the Trinity. o The experiences of healing that you have received in regard to your Blocks and Wounds. Note: most Blocks and Wounds are healed in stages or progressive phases. o Your experience of the Deepening Discovery Exercises, viewing your Blocks through your Longing for deeper intimacy with God.
- As the listener:
  - O Ask clarifying questions with empathy. o What can you gently affirm in the your Companion's sharing?
  - O Delicately ask how your Companion is seeking to take the next step in their healing.
  - O Help your Companion discern the options available to them and the Lord's leading for their healing.

5. Mutual Support, Sharing & Prayer: (30 minutes)

- Pray for one another in the joys and struggles related to this session and for any current prayer requests.
- Closing Prayer: Please read aloud together, followed by your own personal closing prayers for this session.

In Your mercy, O Lord! Be our Rock and our Refuge, the God of all comfort, as we identify and seek to remove those things in our lives that have hindered us from trusting Your love, and pursuing our Longings. Protect us from the schemes and strategies of the evil one to keep us from Your love.

Bring Your light and truth into our hearts and lives. Grant us the courage to forgive ourselves and others. Grant us, to dare to see and accept that we are Your beloved. Help us acknowledge the deep desire of our hearts to desire more of You. Grant us the permission to allow ourselves to long for more of You. And where we are not able, send caring and skilled helpers into our lives. Help us believe that it is worth the risk of facing our pain to know Your love. Help us trust in Your love. This we pray in the name of our Good Heavenly Father, waiting for us with open arms, in the name of the Son, who entered, bore and shares all our sorrows, and in the name of the Holy Spirit, our Comforter and Counselor in every trial. Amen.

- Confirm the next two sessions (time/location).

Additional Resources:

- Seek out a good, recommended Christian counselor, or spiritual director to accompany you through the healing process.
- Brené Brown, *Daring Greatly*.
- Peter Scazzero, *Emotionally Healthy Spirituality*
- C. S. Lewis, *The Great Divorce*. We have already suggested this book in the Longing section, but it explores the hindrances to living in love with God, and various paths of freedom to living into our Longing.
- C. S. Lewis, *The Screwtape Letters*. These letters from a demonic mentor reveals the often hidden schemes and strategies of the evil one to keep us from a life of love with God.
- Brennan Manning, *Abba's Child*
- Brennan Manning, *Ruthless Trust*
- Henri Nouwen, *Life of the Beloved*
- Henri Nouwen, *The Way of the Heart*
- Gerald G. May, *The Awakened Heart: Opening Yourself to the Love You Need*
- Gerald G. May, *Addiction & Grace: Love and Spirituality in the Healing of Addictions*
- Alcoholics Anonymous

If you need and desire some more help, many have found the following ministries helpful. There are a number "healing prayer ministries out there, but we cannot of course recommend one ministry or vet every facilitator of that ministry. Many have found such ministries harmful, such that they need "healing prayer from their healing prayer." While we want to encourage you to believe God for miracles, we also desire that you "trust the long, slow work of God." Short-term seminars or prayer sessions may not be able to help heal Blocks and Wounds that were years in the making. Most often the long-term, holistic approach of a Christian counselor or therapist is most helpful.

Most importantly, you need a safe place where you have the permission to be truly honest with yourself and God. You need permission to be angry that the Longing you have for a deeper, more intimate relationship with Jesus won't and can't develop overnight, but may take many, many years of healing. And that is perfectly okay. God is incredibly patient. With all those caveats and cautions in mind here are a few more suggestions:

- o   The Daring Way™ http://brenebrown.com/ Melanie Saint James (Melanie@imagochristi.org) is a trained, certified facilitator for The Daring Way™ and Rising Strong™ workshops. In *Rising Strong* Brené Brown writes: "in order for forgiveness to happen, something has to die." For some, what has to die is the dream and expectation that they would ever be apart of a normal, happy, and healthy family. Forgiveness often requires that we give up dreams and expectations - and rarely does this death occur quickly and painlessly. Instead, forgiveness of ourselves, others, and even God can be a long process. Too often in the church we seem to hint at a forgiveness happening immediately and therefore we wonder why the pain doesn't magically go away. Forgiveness requires us to keep telling our story, and as we do that our story will begin to lose some of its heat, and as that happens we begin to heal. Healing for most of us, though, is a slow, messy process.

- o   Immanuel Approach. http://www.immanuelapproach.com/ Roy Graham (Roy@imagochristi.org) is experienced in this approach.

o Inner Healing Prayer with Psalm 46 by Bill Gaultiere: http://www.soulshepherding.org/2013/02/inne-healing-prayer-with-psalm-46/)

o Ministries of Pastoral Care. https://ministriesofpastoralcare.com/ based on the work of Leanne Payne).

o Desmond Tutu, *The Book of Forgiving*. This paradigm changing book looks at the reconciliation and forgiveness process after Apartheid in South Africa. In this book, he outlines a fourfold process we must practice and experience in order for forgiveness to take place in our lives. This is both amazingly simple and terribly complex all at the same time, because forgiveness demands that we never pick up our weapons to hurt one another again and because he believes that at the end of forgiveness is the decision we have to make to either continue in the relationship or to let it die.

Session 5: A Journey of Longing through the Paradigm

SESSION PREPARATION

Goals:

- To gain deeper insights into the deepening Love for God that He has planted in your heart.
- To respond to God's call to deeper intimacy with Him through deeper expressions of love with and for God in prayer.
- To build spiritual community through sharing the journey of your Longings.
- To hear and affirm each other's unique journey into deeper intimacy with God through Jesus in the Spirit.

Abiding Prayer Exercises:

1. Choose a Scripture passage that contains the relational metaphor in your Longing Statement to use with the first "Deepening Discovery Exercise" below. (Or utilize a passage listed for your Home Mansion under "Scriptural Support" at the bottom of the Mansions Overview table (Discovery Workbook v.10e2, pp. 32-33)).
2. Psalm 84
3. Ephesians 3:14-19
4. John 15:4-5, 7-10
5. Song of Solomon 2:1, 4, 10-13, 16

Deepening Discovery Exercises:

1.   Abiding Prayer in your Mansion. Reflect on the Abiding Prayer Exercise done above based on a Scripture passage that contains the relational metaphor in your Longing Statement, or from the passages listed for your Home Mansion under "Scriptural Support" at the bottom of the Mansions Overview table (Discovery Workbook v.10e2, pp. 32-33).
   - Which parts of this passage strike you the most? Why?

- How does this passage reflect your experience of this Mansion?
- What are the greatest joys and frustrations about your current Mansion?
- What is your experience of God is unique to this Mansion?

2.   Review your Longing Statement in light of the Teresian Mansion Paradigm:

a.   What is the relational metaphor in your Longing Statement? How could it better express your Longing for deeper relationship with the Lord than you are currently experiencing on a regular basis?

- Look over the characteristics and passages related to your Home Mansion and your Succeeding Mansion. Is there another image you might use that captures the essence of this Longing? Try another image to express your Longing. What aspect of your Succeeding Mansion does it capture that your original Longing Statement did not?

- Rewrite or rephrase your Longing to include elements of your Succeeding Mansion that you long to experience.

3.   Review Movements of Growth Exercise (Discovery Workbook v.10e2, pp. 34-41), and the aspects you underlined:

a.   Which of the Movements of Growth in your Home Mansion seem to be most significant for your future growth? In what way?

- Which of the Movements of Growth from your Previous Mansion may need particular attention for you to "close out" that Mansion?

- What aspect/s of your Spiritual Formation Plan might need more emphasis or clarity, based on these reflections?

- How might you make your Spiritual Formation Plan more challenging or more specific in that area?

4.   Your Journey of Prayer and Longing through the Mansions:

    a. How has the nature of your prayer life changed over the Mansion Journey represented in your Timeline? (Refer to "Nature of Prayer" in Discovery Workbook, v. 10e2, pp. 32-33, and "Prayer" on pp. 34-40).

    o In what ways have you noticed that your capacity for love and human relationship have expanded throughout your Timeline, as you have grown in intimacy with God along your Mansion Journey?

    o How have the Abiding Prayer Exercises in Meditation, Wordless Prayer and Contemplation and Silence during these weeks with the Discovery Companion Exercises encouraged, or stretched your experience of God's love in Abiding Prayer?

COMPANIONS MEETING FOR SESSION 5:

1. Before you begin:

    - Complete the Abiding Prayer and Deepening the Discovery Exercises with enough time for reflection prior to meeting.
    - Allow 1-1/2 to 2 hours for this session.
    - Review the Goals for this session.
    - Bring: Timeline, Discovery Manual, Journal, Bible, and Calendar (for scheduling your next session).

2. Opening Prayer: Please read aloud together, followed by your own personal prayers for this session.

    Lord God we bow before You, the Father, who in love has adopted us into Your heavenly family. Grant us, Lord Spirit, according to the riches of Your glory, to be strengthened with power in the inner man for this journey in deepening intimacy with You. Lord Christ, dwell in our hearts through faith, root and ground us in Your love, so that we may be able to comprehend and experience the dimensions of Your love that surpasses knowledge. Transform us by this journey of intimacy, so that more and more we may know You in Your fullness and experience the greater fullness of fellowship in and with You, the Triune God. Amen.

3. Abiding Prayer Exercise: Ephesians 3:14-19 (10-15 minutes).

    Choose one person to both read the text aloud (3x) and keep track of time. Afterwards, sit with God in silence for 1-2 minutes. We invite you to briefly share the following (about 5 minutes each):

    - Did any specific words or images from the text—or in response to the text—seem to speak to you?
    - What did you experience?
    - What did you feel? (What was your physical, emotional and/or spiritual response?)
    - In what ways do you think you may have experienced Jesus?

4. Sharing your Journey of Longing through the Mansions Paradigm: (40-60 minutes)

    ● Give each Companion 20-30 minutes to share your discoveries during the Deepening Discovery Exercises.
    ● As the speaker, focus your sharing on (one or two of the following):
        o   What were the Mansion implications or changes that the Mansions inspired for your Longing Statement?
        o   What were some of the most significant insights on your Timeline when viewed through the Mansion Paradigm?
        o   How does your current experience of Abiding Prayer reflect your journey through the Mansions?
        o   Which Movements of Growth are most significant for your future growth and your future Spiritual Formation Plan?
    ● As the listener:
        o   Ask clarifying questions.
        o   What can you affirm in the speaker's journey through the Mansions? o Ask your Companion how they hope to intentionally engage their journey based on the Mansion Paradigm.
        o   Help your Companion discern how to take concrete steps towards their Longing that fit their place in the journey through the Mansions.

5. Mutual Support, Sharing & Prayer: (30 minutes)

- Pray for one another in the joys and struggles related to this Module and for any current prayer requests.
- Closing Prayer: Please read aloud together, followed by your own personal closing prayers for this session.

O Lord, so often we have felt lost, even after You found us! The journey of life is about love, but we have made it about lesser substitutes: popularity, sex, power or success. You are Love. You are the source of all love, as the Creator of all that is truly good. You are the initiator of love in your great, life-giving sacrifice for our redemption. You are the goal of Love in the eternal community of the Trinity. You are the pathway of love; in your love, we know Love. Help us journey into Your love; the Love that is You. In Your love, let us learn to love You unconditionally, not for the blessings, power or healing You give, but for Yourself. Teach us to trust Your Love, even when we cannot feel it, or find You; Teach us to reach out for You, to draw our life from You, to live in the power and guidance of Your Love. We pray to You, the Holy Community of Love, Father, Son and Spirit, Amen.

- Confirm the next two sessions (time/location).

Additional Resources:

- R. Thomas Ashbrook, *Mansions of the Heart*, Jossey-Bass, 2009.
- R. Thomas Ashbrook with Ted Wueste, *Mansions of the Heart Study Guide*, 2014.
- The Teresian Mapping Tool, an *Imago Christi* coached assessment and training available at: www.imagochristi.org/mapping-tool/.
- Teresa of Avila, *Interior Castle*.
- Gillian T. W. Ahlgren, *Entering Teresa of Avila's Interior Castle, a reader's companion.* Paulist Press, 2005.
- Thomas Dubay, *Fire Within*, Ignatius Press, 1989.

Session 6: Longing and Spiritual Community

SESSION PREPARATION

Goals:

- To hear and feel God's heart for spiritual community.
- To recognize our need for healthy spiritual community.
- To discern healthy boundaries regarding our current spiritual community.
- To ground our motivations for spiritual community in love.
- To intentionally pursue healthy spiritual community.

Abiding Prayer Exercises

1. John 17:20-24 (in connection with Exercise 1 below)
2. Ephesians 4:1-4
3. Ephesians 4:11-16 (with Exercise 2 below)
4. Romans 12:3-8
5. Matthew 18:19-20

Deepening Discovery Exercises:

Spiritual Community is much more than a useful tool for helping individual Christians to grow into mature saints. Jesus' High Priestly Prayer in John 17 reveals His desire is that we have the same oneness *with each other* that He has with the Father.

At the very heart of the nature of God is the Trinitarian communion of love given, reciprocated, and shared between Father, Son and Holy Spirit. God is love in His very essence. As beings created in the image of God, this same communal love must be at the core of the body of Christ.

Loving God with all our heart, soul, mind and strength, has always been God's first priority and commandment for us. Jesus then taught and empowered us to walk in that love toward God and others. Then He commissioned us to make disciples to obey all that he commanded. Why? Because He has called us to be like Him, as individual persons and as a body. These ever-expanding concentric circles of His love bond us each of us to Him, and in Him each of us to one another. This is the Kingdom of God coming from heaven to earth.

A healthy spiritual community walks in the manner of Jesus. As we walk in humility, gentleness, patience, forbearing love, and eager to maintain the unity of the Spirit in the bond of peace, we begin to experience God being over all, through all, and in all (see Ephesians 4:1-4). A healthy spiritual community nurtures abiding in the love of Jesus *together,* so that loving God with all our heart, mind, soul and strength is just as true for the community *as a whole*, as it is for its individual members.

A communion of love is the very nature of the One in whose image humanity was made. We do not love one another **for God**. We love one another **with God.**

Exercise 1: Hearing God's Longing for us to become one.

Complete the Abiding Prayer Exercise: John 17:20-24 (5-10 min). Then, sit in stillness for 20 minutes with your attention drawn to the Lord. Afterwards, engage the following questions.

- o   In what ways do you think Jesus wants us to be one as He and the Father are one?
- o   What type of Longing does Jesus' prayer stir in you for Spiritual Community?
- o   How does his Longing help you see yourself as an integral member of one Body perfected in unity with the Father, Son, and Holy Spirit, and each other?
- o   In what ways are you feeling drawn or resistant to this calling into His oneness?

After your Abiding Prayer Exercise, take our your Timeline, and:

- Look for patterns of when the pressing needs and busyness of ministry has crowded out the time needed for abiding in healthy spiritual community. What might you need to say "no" to, in order to intentionally pursue the healthy spiritual relationships for which your heart longs?

- Compare the times when you went solo with the times you were paired with someone who needed your gifts and you needed theirs.

- At what season in your Timeline did Community serve to strip away your self-interest in order to serve others, resulting in spiritual flourishing?

- At what season did your serving result in either burnout or foster consumerism in others?

- Spiritual community is highly useful for doing the Lord's work. But when we, as an individual or as a community, start doing **for Him**, rather than **with Him**, we have taken a different yoke and are on the road to burnout. Compare the times when you sacrificially gave **for the Lord** and when you sacrificially gave **with the Lord**.

- Make note of those relationships that flourished in the unity of the Spirit. Take a few moments to soak in some cherished memories. Hold them in your heart before the Lord and give thanks. If there are no good memories of spiritual community, hold up your empty hands before the Lord and ask Him to take hold of one hand, and to send someone to take hold of the other.

- Journal any thoughts on any of these and other insights, challenges, or longings.

Exercise 2: Touching the Spirit-breathed Longing of your heart for healthy spiritual community.

Complete the Abiding Prayer Exercise on Ephesians 4:11-16. Then, be still and attentive before the Lord (20 min.), using the following questions to guide your meditation:

- How do you receive this passage differently in light of a community perspective rather than just an individual one?
- What was your emotional response? Was there confusion, disbelief, anger, hurt, peace, surprise?
- How does your Longing for union with the Lord resonate with the longing for deeper spiritual community?
- When you gather with other Christians, how do you sense the reality of Jesus' presence in your midst (Matthew 18:20)?
- Ask the Lord what areas of growth in community that He desires for you to intentionally pursue.
- Ask Him what gifts He has placed within you to help the fellowship to embrace Jesus' presence. How does your heart respond to this?
- In your personal spiritual community with the Lord, ask for the ears to hear His humility, gentleness, patience, and forbearing love towards you. Ask Him for ears to hear His love when he speaks truth to you, binding your wounds with His peace. How did you emotionally respond to this?
- Ask for the grace to be a vessel of his love and peace when other members of your spiritual community are being difficult. How did you emotionally respond to this?
- Journal on your longing for healthy spiritual community and your emotional response.
- Ask the Lord for the grace to walk in His love and be a vessel of His peace with others.

COMPANIONS MEETING FOR SESSION 6:

1. Before you begin:

    ● Complete the "Deepening the Discovery Exercises" with enough time for reflection prior to meeting.
    ● Allow 1-1/2 to 2 hours for this session.
    ● Review the Goals for this session.
    ● Review Peer-Coaching Principles (see p. 6).
    ● Bring: Timeline, Discovery Manual, Journal, Bible, and Calendar (for scheduling your next session).

2. Opening Prayer: Please read aloud together, followed by your own personal prayers for this session.

    > O Lord, You prayed for Your disciples saying, 'Holy Father, keep them in Your name, the name which You have given Me, that they may be one even as We are. I do not ask for these alone, but for those also who believe in Me through their word; that they may all be one; even as You, Father, are in Me and I in You, that they also may be in Us, so that the world may believe that You sent Me.' Lord, You have brought us together now to be united in You in a very special way for this season. As Spiritual Companions, we know that "Where two or three gather in My name, there am I with them." We thank You for Your presence with us and for the great gift of relationship with You and with one another. Help us be good listeners to each other's heart for You, and to Your heart for each one of us. Guide our conversation by Your Spirit, lead us on the path that draws us ever nearer to You, and sanctify us in Your truth. Amen.

3. Abiding Prayer Exercise: (15-20 minutes)

- Ignatian Reading of John 17:20-24 (5 min)

  In this Ignatian Exercise, we will revisit Jesus' High Priestly Prayer. Imagine this scene from the perspective of one of the characters in the story. Perhaps you will choose to be one of one of the Disciples, Jesus, The Father, The Spirit, or perhaps a personification of God's love or unity.

  Experience the story from the perspective of that person. Hear the passion in Jesus' voice. Are you surprised? Shocked? Confused? Drawn? Fulfilled? Smiling? Frowning? Hear and feel his heart. Look at those around you in the scene. Are you looking at feet or faces? Does this oneness even seem possible? Do they even desire it? Do you find yourself leaning into Jesus' as he prays, or pulling back? What are you feeling?

- Quick share for this this exercise: (5 minutes each)

  Each companion is to briefly share what you experienced and your emotional response. Get in touch with the movement within your heart. (Save those wonderful theological insights for another time and place.)

- Share experiences and insights from Exercises 1-3. (40 min; 20 min each)

- Share your responses from one or more questions from each of the exercises that spoke to your longing for community.

- How did you experience Jesus' longing for us to be one as He and the Father are one? What is your emotional response to this?

- Share your current longing for spiritual community. How is it changing? How will you act on it?

4.   Mutual Support, Sharing & Prayer: (30 minutes)

- Pray for one another in the joys and struggles related to this session and for any current prayer requests.

- Closing Prayer: Have your Companion lead this responsive prayer. (Note: These can also be used as a Breath Prayer.)

  Lead: Father Almighty, Maker of heaven and earth.
  Response: Set up Your Kingdom in our midst.

  Lead: Lord Jesus Christ, Son of the living God:
  Response: Have mercy on me, a sinner.

  Lead: Holy Spirit, Breath of the living God:
  Response: Renew me and all the world.

  Lead: Father, make us one:
  Response: Even as You and Jesus are One.

- Confirm the Closing Session (time/location).

Additional Resources:

- Mindy Caliguire, *Spiritual Friendship*

- Michael Card, *The Walk*

Closing Session:
Discovery Companions in Transition

SESSION PREPARATION

Goals:
- To revise your Spiritual Formation Plan
- To evaluate the Discovery Companions experience
- To bless one another in your ongoing journey of spiritual formation in the love of God.

Abiding Prayer Exercises

1. Matthew 11:25-30
2. Romans 6:5-11
3. Colossians 3:1-17
4. Ephesians 1:15-22
5. Ephesians 3:14-21

Deepening Discovery Exercises

1. Review any changes you made to your spiritual Timeline, your Longing Statement, or in your understanding of your place in the spiritual journey (Teresian paradigm), as you participated in the previous Sessions. Read through the Appendices 1-4 in the Discovery Workbook (v.10e2, pp. 61-78). Identify the spiritual practices you would like to explore further, and possibly include in your next Spiritual Formation Plan.

2. Create a new Spiritual Formation Plan (next page) for the next three-month period. As in the Discovery we recommend that you begin by setting goals in some of the four areas listed below. Set realistic, but also challenging goals. You do *not* have to set a goal in for each of these. Remember that your spiritual growth begins with God and that Jesus is already at work. Cooperate with the Holy Spirit in the creation of the revised plan. Be ready to share your plan with your Companion.

MY SPIRITUAL FORMATION PLAN   Date: _____

Understanding that God desires me to live in loving intimacy with Him and that His purpose is to transform my fallen nature into His own Christ-likeness, first in relationship with the Father and then in daily life, I have identified the following image of the "Longing of my Heart" for deeper relationship with my Lord.

_____

_____

I want to live into this longing by responding to God intentionally through the following Spiritual Formation Plan:

- I will address the following Blocks or Wounds that have kept me from living into my Longing:

- I will offer God the following study or reading to teach me more about my place in the Journey:

- I offer God the following disciplines and schedule as a particular way of responding to God's call to me to greater intimacy with Him in this place in my journey.

- I will seek and foster the following form of spiritual community to help me authentically respond to God.

I will evaluate and revise this plan on _____, having shared it

with_____ for support and accountability.
      I ask God for His grace to help me fulfill this plan in response to His First Order Calling on my life.

Signature: _____   Date: _____

3. Discovery Companions Evaluation: Each of you will have 5 minutes during your Closing Session together to express words of encouragement for your Discovery Companion.

- What do you appreciate most about your Companion?
- What have you gained the most from your Companion?
- What is one thing you will always remember about your Discovery Companion, or be thankful for about your Discovery Companion?
- What were some of the highlights and lowlights of your Discovery Companion Exercises with each other?
- Reconciliation and resolution.
- What is your greatest wish and prayer for your Companion?

4. Consider the possibilities and your preferences for continuing your relationship with your Discovery Companion: For example, you may prefer to:

- o Continue meeting monthly for a while

- o Check in with one another in 6 months, or

- o Email a monthly note of encouragement or journal update.

- o Other: _____

5. We would love to hear about your experience. What worked well? What might help to improve the process? Please contact us via email at info@imagochristi.org.

COMPANIONS MEETING FOR CLOSING SESSION:

1. Before you begin:

    - Complete the "Abiding Prayer Exercises" and "Deepening the
      Discovery Exercises" with enough time for reflection prior to
      meeting.
    - Please contact *Imago Christi* via email at info@imagochristi.org
      to let us know that you are finishing the *Exercises for Discovery
      Companions.*
    - Allow 1-1/2 to 2 hours for this session.
    - Review the Goals for this session.
    - Bring: Timeline, Spiritual Formation Plan, Discovery Manual,
      Journal, and your Bible.

2. Opening Prayer: Please read aloud together, followed by your own
    personal prayers for this session.

    O Lord, it is with great thanksgiving that we come to You today. We are
    so grateful for this opportunity to engage with one another as Your
    disciplines. You give us great assure that our fellowship with one another
    is important when You said, " For where two or three are gathered in my
    name, there am I among them." Thank You for being with us and for
    giving us fellow believers who share our journey and help us become
    who You intend for us to be. We offer to You our time together and invite
    Your Holy Spirit to help us and to guide us into an ever-deepening
    relationship with You.

3. Abiding Prayer Exercise: 2 Peter 1:4-11 (10-15 minutes).

   Choose one person to both read the text aloud (3x) and keep track of time. Afterwards, sit with God in silence for 1-2 minutes.
   We invite you to briefly share the following (about 5 minutes each).

   - Did any specific words or images from the text—or in response to the text—seem to speak to you?
   - What did you experience?
   - What did you feel?
   - What was your physical, emotional and/or spiritual response?
   - In what ways do you think you may have experienced Jesus?

4. Discovery Companions Debrief:

   a. Sharing Spiritual Formation Plan Revisions:
      i.   Give each Companion 10 minutes to share their revised Spiritual Formation Plan.
      ii. Focus sharing on:
           - Any changes made to your Spiritual Formation Plan
           - Take time to go into deeper explanation on any or all of the items, perhaps pausing after each section to allow the companion to ask questions

   b. Discovery Companions Evaluation: Give each Companion 5 minutes to express encouragement about their Discovery Companion.

      - What do you appreciate most about your Companion?
      - What have you gained the most from your Companion?
      - What is one thing you will always remember about your Discovery Companion, or be thankful for about your Discovery Companion?
      - What were some of the highlights and lowlights of your Discovery Companion Exercises with each other?
      - What is your greatest wish and prayer for your Companion?

5. Mutual Support, Sharing & Closing Prayer:

- Take time to bless one another and to cover these new Spiritual Formation Plans with prayer.
- Pray for any current prayer requests.
- Discuss your preferences for continuing your relationship with your Discovery Companion: For example, you may prefer to:
  - Continue meeting monthly for a while
  - Check in with one another in 6 months, or
  - Email a monthly note of encouragement or journal update.
  - Other (your suggestion)

- A Blessing from the *Imago Christi* Core Community. Afterwards, please feel free to add your own personal closing prayers of thanksgiving. Read in unison:

  O Lord, You have placed a deep desire for greater intimacy with You within these Discovery Companions. You have blessed them in their journey together as Companions these weeks and months. Bless their continued journeying in Your love with Your presence and an ever-deepening attentiveness to You in love. Let their lives be so transformed in Your likeness, that all of their service in Your Name flows out of their love for You, and invites others into the love they enjoy with You. This we pray in the Name of the Father, the Son, and the Holy Spirit. Amen.

Additional Resources:

- Adele Calhoun, *Spiritual Disciplines Handbook: Practices That Transform Us.*

- Richard J. Foster, *Celebration of Discipline.*

- If you long for more people in your church, ministry or missions context to share the language and the tastes of spiritual formation that you have experienced in Discovery, consider hosting an *Imago Christi* Spiritual Formation Discovery event in your town. Contact us via email: info@imagochristi.org for more information.

Made in the USA
Columbia, SC
10 October 2018